SHIPPING CONTAINER HOMES

The Complete Guide to Understanding Shipping Container Homes

Richard Nelson

Table of Contents

Introduction

For many of us the idea of building our home is a dream we've often indulged in – imagining how we would have the rooms laid out, making sure the space that was important to us got the most attention, and just thinking how we'd do our homes in our own way.

However, practicality usually gets in the way; you need lots of land and most of the good stuff is taken, it requires lots of materials and skills, and it will take a great deal of time going from the planning stage to putting your feet up in a lounge room of your own design.

There are solutions to these problems though that won't cost a fortune and can make your dream a reality. What if you built a home that didn't take up that much space? What if you built a home out of an already existing structure that could be purchased cheaply?

As you might be able to guess from the title of this book, shipping containers may just be one answer to the 'build your own home' dilemma.

Ex-shipping containers have been used for many years for various purposes including storage and makeshift shelters, but since the rise in popularity of minimalism the prospect of making one your home has become more inviting as people begin to care less for space to store things they don't need.

Making a shipping container into a home you can live in or an office you can work out is not quite as simple as it seems. You need to get hold of a shipping container, get it into place, have the correct planning permission, get the timing done correctly, and you need to have your plans in place before you begin doing any of that.

Thankfully with the help of the internet and books such as this making a shipping container into your home or a place of work is viable project and we're here to help you consider whether a shipping container home is for you, how to get started, how to overcome the obstacles of finding the right land, getting plans together and finding the right team to help, designing a home that suits you with some of our sample plans, and finally how to put everything into place.

Welcome to your new home.

What is a shipping container?

Let's begin with what might seem to be too obvious: what exactly is a shipping container? Or, to be more precise, what kind of shipping container can be used to actually build a house?

You know that a shipping container is the big metal box that is used to ship large quantities of goods across the open sea. This means they are durable and built to have considerable amounts of goodies stored in them. It also means they are built to be moved around fairly easily, they can be stacked on top of each other with ease (although the sides themselves can be relatively weak), and they are suitable for transportation.

They vary in size from 8 ft to 40 ft long with a typical height and width of 8 ft to 9 ft. They come in a variety of types and materials. On the cheap end you can get wooden crates and on a more expensive level they might contain powerful cooling or refrigeration units inside. The most durable containers are known as COR-TEN steel containers and are especially sturdy in heavy weather conditions (gales and salt water).

When buying them you will have a choice of whether you want a new, refurbished, used, or a very used model. Some containers can be used for long as 20 years and can be purchased cheaply with the knowledge they will be beat-up when they arrive. You can purchase some that have only been on a single trip (typically from China) and may have some damage, but otherwise should be in fairly good condition.

The appeal of many containers is how open to modification they are and the fact you can work on them off-site and then have them carted in to be placed on a foundation and quickly finished off for living in. Prices vary from as little as $1,000 for an old container to as much as $9,000 for a container that comes with some modification making it nearly fit for living.

Prices of shipping containers in recent times have become quite cheap as the USA has declined in their use of them and the fact that it's often cheaper to send a new one from Asia than to ship back an empty one to be used again.

These prices are generally before modifications and before shipping, and you will need modifications on the basic shipping container. Before buying one you should be able to inspect it or have it inspected by others to ensure it is weatherproof and sealable.

Do shipping containers make good homes?

On the surface it would seem that shipping containers are an ideal building material for a home. They may only be 320 square foot (which is miniscule compared to the average US home size of 2,600 square foot), but you can put a few together or stack them up to quickly double, triple, or quadruple that size.

The size can also be very efficiently used with open plan living, no stairs, and by using the roof as an easy porch. The structures are fairly solid and stable and they are built to be weather proof. But you may have noticed that not many houses are built out of shipping containers.

Partly this is because people want bigger houses which are generally easier to accomplish with bricks after a certain point, and the boxy aesthetic hasn't always been appreciated. The real truth, however, is that the advantage of a shipping container isn't that they are cheap or particularly well-suited to being turned into a house.

Being a box made for storage they need to be reshaped and cut-up before you can get in and out of them. They are weather-proof, but not well insulated and so they need to have walls reinforced and padded. The floors are made to be rodent resistant which means they are treated with poison and need to be stripped out and replaced. And, finally, they can be quite noisy and oscillate between being too cold or too hot.

This isn't too put you off a shipping container home because there are advantages to using them as building materials. But, the primary reason for anyone choosing to build a shipping container home should be because they love the look, and they want to build an easy to maintain and smaller stylish home.

Will a shipping container save me money?

At $3,000 dollars it might seem a cheap option considering many of the materials are there and you won't require as much building to get them into shape. However, get two containers and you are already at $6,000 and the basic materials for a home might not be as pricey as you think if you are happy with a smaller living space.

$6,000, that is, before you've done anything significant to the containers or had them dropped into place on a foundation. The average cost of building a house is $300,000, but a low cost build can be as little as $26,000.

Shipping container homes definitely come in at the lower-cost end of building a home, but they should be seen as an alternative choice to a standard brick-and-mortar house and not as some kind of money saving hack. Having a home you will live in comfortably built for $26,000 is extremely tricky.

Let's quickly have a look at the costs and how they might break down for the average home. $3,000 is a lower estimate for the price of a typical shipping container, but even so that is just the basic cost. Once you start cutting sides off or putting doors into a container the walls needs to be reinforced.

It might seem that a shipping container would have an incredibly durable structure that could take a lot of strain and battering, but that's only so long as they are used for their original purpose. They are made to be stacked one on top of the other where supports are in place. The containers are heavy; heavier than many regular houses are, and you need to be sure each side will stay up one you start cutting chunks out. Nevertheless, once you have done this it will be a very sturdy house in comparison to many low-cost houses.

In many ways part of the appeal of a shipping container is that it's possible to cut out a side yourself if you felt inclined to do so and you had the right kind of saw at your disposal.

Once you have put in windows and doors, and re-done the floors and put in a roof that won't collect too much water you then need to transport the thing and lay it on a foundation. After that you need to attach plumbing, electricity, and heating – which need to be done in a smaller space than a conventional home.

This work will need to be done on however many containers you have if you want to keep them as separate units (though building a double-wide container comes with its own difficulties). If you live in a very hot or very cold climate it's likely that you will need to significantly alter the appearance of the container to make sure it is comfortably inhabitable.

To the extent that you might not recognize you have a shipping container any longer once the roof and sides are put in. For a cold climate extra insulation will be necessary and in hot climates more space will be required for ventilation ducts. If not prepared properly then containers can get very hot and are prone to humidity and moisture. While shipping containers are generally very good at being weather-resistant, too much moisture inside can make them go rusty fairly quickly.

Working on a shipping container will sometimes require more specialist work than a house with a wooden frame, but if you can do some of the work yourself then there is of course money to be saved (although not anymore than if you worked on a standard house).

Coming up with a number that will fit all needs is impossible, but speaking in general terms, shipping costs can be between $3,000 to $10,000 (you can save money by shipping more at once); plumbing and electricity might cost $10,000 (but a lot can be saved here if you do it yourself); preparing the site and laying a foundation might cost around $12,000; building in furniture, putting in doors and glass, and finishing the inside might cost you as much as $20,000; and, finally, the cost of labor can range from $50 to $200 an hour with possibly 100 or more hours of work required.

Not including land and for a very basic two container home you are looking at a price of around $60,000. That is a low estimate and assumes you'll be very hands on. It is also much cheaper than a standard home.

In addition, there are many ways to save money on these homes. In certain locations you can forgo laying a foundation depending on the building regulations and the grounds. You can purchase a container that is already finished and ready for wiring and plumbing for as little as $20,000 in some instances. If the weather is mild you might be able to get away with a very basic roof or less insulation.

If you are interested in a more off-the-grid style of living you might be content with a gas cooker, using portable electric heaters, and having outdoor plumbing. This would require little more than the house to be wired for electricity which in a simple home is not a hugely tricky job.

You might want to have a shipping container as office space or extra living space next to an already built home which will mean it doesn't have to be quite as self-contained.

Good planning is crucial to saving money and is a place where a shipping container can come into its own. If you have as much done off-site as possible and get a larger team of builders and workers ready, then a container home can be shipped over and put up in a matter of days.

This can significantly cut down on the cost of building a home and it can save you extra money when moving from one house to the next (to avoid being stuck paying to build a house and to live in another for too long).

Why bother with a shipping container?

It's reasonable to ask at this point, why bother with a shipping container home? They can lend themselves to be cheap, especially if you aren't looking for a luxurious long-term home, but it's unrealistic to think they are cheaper than a conventional home of a similar size or complexity.

They're often pitched as a way of getting a cheap home, but if that's not the case then you just left with a home that's maybe a bit less practical and spacious than a wooden-framed house?

Firstly, it seems unlikely that you are reading this simply because you thought shipping container homes were cheap. If you merely wanted a cheap boxy home, then you could buy a second-hand trailer house and be living in it by the end of the week.

The shipping container home offers two main things. The first is that it offers a stylish and highly customizable home relatively cheaply. When you look at many tiny homes or eco-homes the first thought that comes to mind isn't "I really want to live in that house," but shipping containers have their own aesthetic that is crisp and sharp. If you want a stylish home, then a shipping container is one of the most affordable ways to do it.

The second main reason is that building a shipping container home can be done very quickly and with a limited amount of space. Building your own home without irritating those around you and without having to individually pay to rent out equipment and have it maneuver around your land can be tricky.

Since you can get a lot of the work done off-site with a shipping container, you can keep your building chaos to a minimum. It will, however, require the use of cranes, which isn't often the case with regular houses.

If you need a home quickly, if you want to just have your home built and ready, or if you are looking for temporary shelter then a shipping container can be the ideal solution.

For others it is just an exciting project to work on and they want to show off their architectural credentials with a recycled shipping container.

The shipping container philosophy

The last few sections have talked about the practicality of a shipping container home but they haven't talked about what's so special about them – why is it that so many people are so excited by them? So let's talk a little about that to get you excited.

The shipping container philosophy is a dual philosophy that considers design and lifestyle.

The shipping container design philosophy

When looking at shipping container design you can think about the aesthetic aspect and the environmental aspect. A shipping container embodies the idea of recycling objects or as it's sometimes known 'upcycling'.

This is because you are literally building your house out of a recycled material and the huge amounts of steel needed for a home don't need to be created and you reduce the use of many other materials. The shipping containers are also ripe for a more sustainable type of living if you keep them small and insulate them well. Since you are taking control of your home you can choose to use solar panel and more environmentally friendly toilets if you wish.

Shipping containers are ideal for off-the-grid living and encourage people to use less when they start preparing them. There is a thin line here between actually being sustainable and fooling yourself into thinking that merely using recycled goods is making an impact on the world; but green housing is an important part of the drive for shipping containers.

If you want to go green with your home, then make sure you are creating huge amounts of waste with a shipping container home.

When it comes to the look of the shipping container it can be confusing at first why architects have taken to them so much recently. After all, a large rectangle is fairly easy to build with a wooden structure and many houses can have large open windows.

Shipping containers do make these sorts of sleek, minimal, and open designs much easier. A cheap wooden frame will often struggle to hold a large glass window, but a shipping container can do it fairly simply. Stacking a container on top of another one creates a fascinating design that can only be done much more artificially with regular building materials.

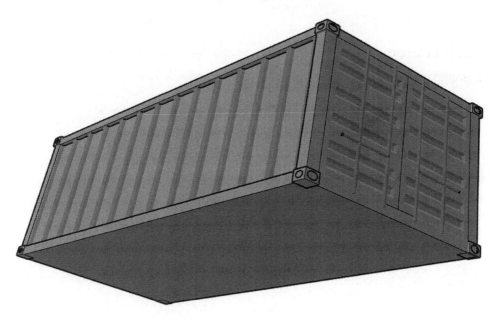

Perhaps most important is the fact that you can place them down with a very simple foundation in almost any environment. If you want to build something with a metal structure and a lot of metal attachments, then a shipping container is one of the simplest ways of achieving this.

Finally, they just offer a look that is undeniably appealing and sexy. A regular house will often end up looking stuffy or generic, but a shipping container will always look unique and force you to use your living space differently.

The shipping container lifestyle philosophy

By their nature shipping containers encourage a minimalist lifestyle because space is at a premium and if you filled a two container house with too much stuff you'd quickly find there was nowhere left for you.

Not only do the sharp and simple lines of a shipping container give a minimalist look, but designing one forces you to ask what do I really need out of a home? Do I need to have six separate rooms for all the different things that I do? In the 21st century we want to start questioning the need to have so many rooms which then require separate furniture.

Sharing space allows you to easily reduce the amount of furniture you have and you can begin to downsize the amount of possessions you have in general. Getting rid of possessions for the sake of having fewer things is not necessarily a brilliant idea, but giving yourself the space to really question what you need to function and be happy can allow you to reassess how you live.

A shipping container can become the embodiment of this change in attitude because the whole project can be catered to your life and built to emphasize the things that matter to you. With large windows and less space, you'll often find you want to use the outside space more. Your kitchen is no longer a hidden away space you have to endure when you are on your own, but instead a social place that can be shared with others.

With enough of a restriction on space you can find that not only do you limit yourself to the things you need but they become decorations in your home as storage becomes more in your face, and you can see them with fresh eyes.

One of the reasons so many people enjoy building their own homes is that they then know where everything goes. When you have any problems, when you want to know where slugs are coming into the kitchen from, and when you are trying to determine if the place is insulated enough – you will know because you know how everything fits together.

Approaches to a shipping container home

Once you've decided you do want to build a shipping container home or building, the first question is going to be what kind of approach are you going to have?

For a conventional house you are somewhat limited in your approaches. You put down a foundation and you start building up from there and bring supplies along as you need them. Then when the house is done you can't do much with it unless you extend it or knock it down and start again.

With a shipping container you have a few different options.

Building on-site

You can build the house on-site either directly on to a foundation or have it moved over when you are ready. This is most like a traditional house and is useful if you have easy access to the land you will be near and getting tools isn't a problem. It means you can work on the house for as long as you like and you can reduce the amount of moving you have to do if you plan ahead.

When buying a shipping container, you will often need to firstly have it delivered to a location and then you move it to the site you plan to erect the house. Going straight to the building site allows you to reduce the amount of moving and makes it a bit safer when you do finally move it into place.

If you are planning to be very involved, you have access to equipment, and you are planning to do a smaller and simpler build then on-site building might be for you. Don't forget though, there might not being anything on your land and you will need power and other utilities to help you build.

Building off-site

Many cities and towns around the world will have off-site workshops that will allow you to rent space there to work and build on a project like a shipping container. The facilities they offer will vary, but you can get one that lets you starting building the place indoors and will give you access to a lot of equipment and tools.

Here things will be safe and you'll have access to everything you need easily. Once you are done with the really heavy lifting and exterior, you then move the container into place and fix the interior and connect all of the wiring and plumbing.

If you plan to build the container yourself then building off-site can be difficult and time consuming. Not only do you need to get out there during work hours but so will any team that you work with. You'll have to pay just to use the facilities and you do actually need to find somewhere that will let you use their space. Many places are more than happy to do the work for you, but they won't necessarily want some untrained and uninsured cowboy turning up and using their space when they could be using it themselves.

Whether or not it is cost effective to build off-site or not will depend on your set-up. The cost of transporting the container and renting the space and use of tools may be a similar price once all things are taken into account. When you work on-site you are guaranteed access to the tools you rent, you can work whenever you want (for however long you want), and there is no worry of making a unit too heavy to move and transport.

Prefabricated home

The third main option is to more-or-less have the shipping container prefabricated by others off-site and then have them in place to finish the wiring and plumbing yourself.

With this option you can have some basic shipping containers converted so they are ready to use but will still require a lot of input from you, you can have them built very close to a specification of your choice, or you can have the containers built to pre-made plans and just put them in place. This option can be very expensive with designer containers (coming with several modified containers) going for as much as $200,000.

However, it can also save a lot of time and energy and may, ultimately, not cost much more than doing it yourself if you lack expertise. Don't forget that your time is worth something – so saving yourself a few hundred hours work and planning might be time you could be earning money.

If you find yourself wanting to have a big role in building the house, then you might want to ask yourself what is really important to you. Do you just want to renovate a home? Do you want a house that meets your specifications? Or do you just want an involved project?

If you're serious about building a long-term home yourself then you will almost certainly need help in some form. The question is how much do you actually want to do yourself?

Very simple container home

This last approach isn't really an option if you are interested in a home to live in full-time, but it's possible to make very simple and cheap shipping container shelters or work space for not much money.

You can buy a finished container with doors and windows for a few thousand dollars (not including delivery). If you have the right kind of ground, you can get away without even having a proper foundation. Building on softer soil will require a hefty foundation, but directly onto concrete or harder ground might require something as simple as a few concrete piers (essentially concrete lumps that hold up your container).

Insulation will be required if you plan to spend much time in this container (as will adequate weather proofing), but if you are at a site that already has electricity or you are happy using a generator you might be able to get away without even properly wiring the container.

This would work for temporary accommodation or if you want a shipping container as an outside office or recreation room. If you were particularly into Spartan style living you could continue to live in your shipping container while you built and modified it and others.

Whichever approach you take to your shipping container you will face many of the same obstacles so in the following book we will work through getting ready to build and help you in making the right decisions when you come to them.

Financing a shipping container home

If you already have giant stacks of money around to buy or build a new home, then you may want to skip this section. If, however, you are planning to sell your home or to find some kind of financing to help you create your shipping container home then shipping containers provide a unique challenge.

Building with a construction loan

Typically, if you wanted to build a home you would try getting a construction loan from your bank. In short you create a timetable for building the home, your plans for having it finished, and give them a budget for the house.

If approved you will then only pay interest on the loan as it is being built, and upon full and final completion this will become a normal home loan where the house works as collateral. You can just get a construction loan (not a single close construction loan which automatically turns into a mortgage), but the interest rates are likely to be higher.

Whether or not you go for a single construction loan or you go for that and a mortgage; a construction loan will usually have higher interest rates. You will also usually need to have a fairly strong banking history to qualify for the loan. There is no real collateral until the house is built which makes it a riskier prospect for the bank.

Of course, the price of construction should be cheaper than simply buying a new and already built home, so the extra interest is not necessarily as much as it first appears. The down payment for a loan like this is typically much higher than the loan for a conventional home mortgage though – sometimes as much as 25% of the total project.

For an individual with no history of building homes getting a construction loan can be difficult. You need to prove very convincingly that your home is going to be built by professionals and it will get done in a reasonable timeframe. You are building it with someone else's money and you can't simply choose to not finish the home.

Shipping container homes take on another dimension of difficult because they are seen as unusual homes by lenders. A lender wants to take the fewest risks possible and they want evidence that what you are building is actually worth something. If there are no shipping container homes in your area that are selling, then there is no evidence it is worth building your home.

Often larger banks will simply not fund this kind of project and you will have to look to smaller banks in your local area that can help with this kind of home. You will need to make sure they have financed other prefabricated or modular homes in your area and work carefully with them to devise a plan that will work for both of you. A private property appraiser may be able to help you if they have experience in the area and direct you towards a suitable lender.

This is where you have to make a big decision if you are planning to sell a home to finance this type of shipping container home as it's not guaranteed that such a property will be worth much in years to come. If you are building this home as a solid investment for the future, you may have to think again.

For many people the best option is to raise a considerable amount of money on your own and then try to get a basic construction loan. This loan often grows as the price of the build grows. Once built you can then have the property appraised property and get finance on that property.

Building without a construction loan

Many people coming to shipping container homes aren't necessarily established home owners with good credit rating. They are looking for the home specifically, because it is cheaper to build and they don't want to go the traditional route.

If you have no banking history and no property to sell, then few banks are going to help you get a construction loan because it is simply too risky for them. This doesn't mean you have to give up on your dream as there are several other options.

The one most similar to a construction loan is to find a construction company that will take care of financing for you. If you find the correct company, they will only require that you have a deposit and a steady income. After that they will finance the building and give you a mortgage for the property when it is complete.

This a good option if you don't want the hassle of doing paperwork for two or three loans and you want to deal with someone that will have a better understanding of what you are doing. The big catch though, is that construction companies are possibly going to be even more conservative than a bank in what they will help finance. If they don't perceive a property as valuable they won't help you finance it.

If that option still presents you with difficulties, then you will need to become more creative. Most of these loans include the cost of land, but if you have access to land you can build on, then things become easier. Construction loans are necessary if you want to build quickly as you need a lot of money at once.

If you are planning on doing more of the work yourself, on-site, and at your own pace then the need for a large loan is not as pressing. You will need to finish the project to ensure you are not wasting money, but taking a year or even two is a better investment if you can avoid paying lots of interest and bypass a serious loan altogether.

If you intend to build on land where you already lived or that is already partly developed, then you will find that many of your costs go down dramatically. What you will need to ensure, especially if you are going to need planning permission to build, is that you have all of the basics in place to lay a container on a foundation and so that you can leave it knowing it will be sealed and weatherproof.

Getting the permissions, the plans, the foundation, the transport, and the shipping container to begin work will mean that you need to have a considerable amount of money upfront.

You can think of this like a down payment on a mortgage and you could cover some of it with a reasonable personal loan (which can have quite competitive interest rates for smaller amounts) or by borrowing the money from family and friends. If you have a home, you might be able to re-finance it again and free up some money that way.

The more you can do yourself the less money you will need to borrow and ultimately pay interest on. For someone without much ability to bring a lot of capital quickly you will need to look into cheaper and recyclable ways of doing things, and you will need to plan a smaller property that accomplished mostly with the tools around. When bringing outside help you will need to work to a very tight and cost-effective plan.

If you currently own a home, you may consider renting it out while you work on your property to raise money and to incentivize you to finish your shipping container home.

When figuring out costs always assume there will be far more costs than you had anticipated whether that is fees for agents, the costs of paperwork, unexpected additions to the property, or just structural or design changes to the property. If you are not confident you can fully finance the project, then it is not wise to begin on the project.

You may still enjoy planning and preparing to build a shipping container home without the right financing ready, but you will need to be sure of this before you go too far ahead.

Your ideal shipping container home

Before going much further with planning and preparing to build your shipping container home you will need to be sure of what your needs and wants are for a home, as well as the resources you already have to hand.

At this stage you do not need to be too specific with your plan, but you should take the time to write down how many rooms you will need including office space, lounge space, bedroom space, and kitchen and bathroom space. On top of that you will have to determine where you need to live and where you want to live.

Write down lists for the amount of space you think you will need and consider mapping that out in your current home to see how large that really would be. Then determine the kind of funding you might be eligible for and how quickly you would need to get a home built.

You may want to do this as you go along reading this book and other resources, but having the basics of where, how big the house needs to be, and your rough timeframe will help you start mentally planning.

Zoning, regulation and permits

Before buying your container or even the land you wish you to build on you will need to be sure you are allowed to build a modular or shipping container home in your chosen area. You should have an idea of where you need to live and you can use this information to start telling you if you can build in that area which will then let you know the kind of land that is available.

As you might have guessed from the lack of shipping container homes in most suburbs, getting your home in the right location is not always that simple.

Different areas of land have different regulated uses whether that is business, industrial, or residential usage. Just because something is an industrial area doesn't mean you can't build a residential home there, but it might be more difficult to achieve. It is possible to apply for a 'variance' which will let you use land in a manner it is not currently zoned for.

After you've found land to buy in an area where you can build a residential property you will need to get permission to connect a home up to sewers and to construct a driveway up to your property. That is after a neighborhood has agreed to allow you to build your chosen property near their homes on the land you are interested in.

All of this can be very costly, especially if you are not well-informed about an area and what you can do with the property. Getting permission for a home that is connected to all the required facilities can cost tens of thousands of dollars and even dwarf the costs of getting things built.

In many locations a smaller building may come under the same category as a shed or garage and getting permission is fairly simple; but, things always become more complicated when you want it to be wired, plumed, and lived in.

Land that already has certain permissions will usually cost more than land without any. You will need to be sure that the land you are interested in (or already own) allows residential homes and doesn't have any restrictions on shipping container homes (or a history of issues with prefabricated or modular homes).

Once you are certain of all that you can make a bid on some land that will only be successful once you have approval from the neighborhood to build there. This is one of the parts of building a shipping container home that are ignored when telling you about how cheap it is to build one.

It can seem terrifying to get all these permissions ready but there are lots of people ready to help you and there is not too much reason to be glum about it. People in the area might appreciate a beautiful looking building near them and welcome you with open arms. You can also sell the fact it will be a quick build that has been chosen to enhance the local area. A shipping contained need not look like a shipping container either, it can be made to look like a far more attractive prospect if given the right kind of accoutrements.

You will often have better luck in rural and more remote locations, as well as places that might be seen as less desirable by some. Let's face it though; you didn't intend to build a shipping container house because you wanted to fit in line with the other boring suburban homes. The further out of a city zoning area the more you can go wild with your architectural inventions.

If you work with a construction company or similar you will find that they are able to take care of a lot of this for you – at a price of course.

Another good option is to use land you already own or is owned by a friend or family member. If you have enough land to work with that is out of the way and you promise the home will look attractive and be mostly out of the way you will have more success than if you try to impose on others from the outside.

Getting the right land for your shipping container home

Shipping container homes are versatile and don't need as much space as many other properties, but you do need to make sure you can get hold of the right type of land in the first place.

You already know what you have to look for in zoning laws but there are different considerations when looking at land to build on. If you aren't buying in rural locations or those outside of restrictive zoning rules, then you'll need to get the help of a realtor to make sure you are looking in the right areas for lots that can be built upon.

The price of land will vary depending on its location and how ready it is to be built upon. Some pieces of land may come with a drive and plumbing in place and building will not take much more than putting your container into place. It will cost more but it might save you a lot in time and effort. You will need to be sure that the ground is suitable for building on and that you won't have to spend too much on bringing it up to a level where you can comfortably build on it.

Be cautious of quickly buying land at auction with investigating it and having a good idea of whether you can use it or not. It might be sensible to have a back-up plan in such an instance if you are not able to create a shipping-container home.

It is wise to consider what the land around the buildable area is like. Shipping containers can be susceptible to lots of noise from wind and other weather, so building on land that is too exposed and has no shelter might end up causing you a headache. Equally you might save money by having a home that is in the shade by reducing the cost of cooling your home.

Lastly try to think about how the land will be for ease of building. At some point you will need a large crane with a shipping container on it to access the land you want to build on. You will want there be an easy way to get a truck near it and to do so without disturbing your neighbors.

Always seek legal advice before purchasing property or land and make sure you have adequate financing ready.

Buying a shipping container

The most important ingredient in the shipping container home is the shipping container itself. Later in the book we will look at some example plans and how you could use them for your own plans and designs.

Before we get there it is important that you understand how a shipping container home takes shape, what your options really are, the limitations you will be dealing with and the costs involved in the different choices you make.

The first step for a lot of builds is which kind of containers you want and how much work you want to put into them.

The first thing you need to determine is where you are going to buy a container from. If live near a port or shipyard you might find you have relatively easy and cheap access to older or even newer shipping containers at good prices. However, it's often difficult to go in and collect a container yourself if you are an outsider and certainly picking one up yourself is difficult without a commercial driver's license.

If you go online or explore local building suppliers, you might find they sell mostly prefabricated containers at a higher price that might not meet your specification. Many do not sell good-value untouched containers, and, after all, why would they? You can just as easily buy a container yourself and it needs to be shipped on to you either way.

However, many sites will sell you an untouched shipping container and it might be the easiest option as they do all the heavy lifting and organization for you. Try to look for sites that sell just the containers rather than prefabricated ones if that is what you are looking for. You'll possibly end up paying more for the unit but it could be money that is worth paying. Be careful with some of these sites as they can often add on quite a few additional costs.

Besides getting a container directly, the cheapest option will often be buying one on eBay or Craigslist. You'll not always have a guarantee that the container you are buying is in good condition and you'll need to organize collection yourself much of the time (part of the reason for the discounts you might find).

Types of storage containers

There are many different types of storage containers to choose from, with different materials, sizes and options.

Sizes usually begin with a 10 ft cube and the most common sizes are 20 ft and 40ft, with options for a higher unit in the 20 and 40 ft sizes (usually 9 to 10-foot-high instead of 8 foot). The weights of the 20ft and 40ft and usually between 5,000 and 8,000 pounds when they are empty and can carry up to 60 or 70,000 pounds of goods.

How big should yours be? The average home has about 1,000 cubic feet worth of furniture which theoretically can fit in a 20-foot container which has a cubic foot storage capacity of about 1,170 feet, but that's for storage and not living and moving around. A 40-foot container has 2,391 foot and a high 40-foot container has 2,700 foot. But remember that is the entirety of the container and not just the space you can easily access.

Different companies and sellers use different lingo when selling the units. If you are buying a used container you will generally find they promise to be wind and water tight and then they will vary in how beat-up, dented, used or worn they are.

Many sellers will list whether they need to be re-painted, cleaned down with a pressure washer. The catch here with the lower priced containers is that having them re-painted or fitted with a door or window can cost as much as the container itself. This additional cost leaves you with the question of whether a painted and re-furbished container is worth $900 or more dollars per container instead of doing it yourself. If you are in a hot country, you may need a special type of paint that keeps the sun at bay better.

You can order new containers from China or Asia, or opt for a one-trip container that has only made one journey. The price of these is often not considerably more than a used one and if you really want a storage container look (rather than a painted unit) these may be the way to go.

The containers may come with a variety of abbreviations. CW and WWT are the most common and they tell you whether a container is Cargo Worthy or if it is Wind & Water Tight. If you are not planning on sending the container across the ocean, then you don't need to pay extra for it to be cargo worthy.

The other specifications tell you if the container has been inspected and improved by a certain body, such as; the Institute of International Container Lessors (IICL), Convention for Safe Containers (CSC), and the Approved Continuous Examination Program (ACEP).

You might also need to know the maximum weight allowable (MGW), the weight of an empty container (known as the Tare), and name of the plate on the front of the container including its serial number (the CSC plate).

Shipping containers are often graded from Certified Containers (that are certified by the above bodies) that are fit for shipping and cost a bit more, to A-Grade containers which are weatherproof and in a solid condition with working doors, B Grade which are heavily worn and mostly weatherproof – though not perfectly so, and finally there are C and D Grade containers which are so damaged that they are being sold for scrap.

The variety of containers is enormous considering all the different things they are made to transport. Some come with huge container doors; some are built like tunnels, or come with roofs that can be easily opened up. There are refrigeration units that are sometimes called 'reefers', and there are insulated containers made to keep the inside dry and warm. The most common you will use for a shipping container home are the dry storage containers.

Insulated containers may seem appealing or a shortcut, but they are not always insulated in a way that is suited to home living so more often than not a basic dry storage container will be the most suitable container for most people. They are also by far the easiest to get hold of.

Standards containers are built out of Corten steel, but specially built containers come in a variety of materials. For most purposes basic Corten steel should be more than adequate.

When you finally decide on what you want to buy make sure that you haggle no matter where you are buying it from (containers are usually in pretty abundant supply) and you may wish to inspect the container before you actually buy it. If you are buying several then it might be worth investing the time in buying a one-trip container straight from China and haggling yourself into a discount.

Shipping of containers will often happen in just a few days after purchasing if you wish so you need to be sure you are ready to have it delivered and you have the supports in place to have them delivered. This means having a foundation, supports, or a trailer that can move a storage container.

You will also need to decide whether you want to have it worked on-site first before you get it delivered. The costs of shipping might mean that buying a container from the place you plan to modify it off-site could save you money – as could buying it largely pre-fabricated.

Doors, walls, and floors

Once you've got a shipping container the question will be how you want to prepare it for living in and how much you need or want to get ready before laying it down on its foundation and working on it.

If you have enough equipment you might be able to work on the container while it is on a trailer and then slide it onto its foundations to finish it off. For most people work will either need to be done off-site or on-site while on the homes foundation.

Doors and windows

If you want to make a home out of a shipping container you will need doors and windows to have natural light and for it to be livable in. Of course, containers naturally come with a door on them, but it's unlikely you'll want to use such a big and unwieldy door any time you want to get in and the options for locking from the inside are not always desirable.

Whether you want to do this part yourself or have the container prefabricated is a question of what kind of design you are going for. If you are going for a very simple home with only one or two containers together then getting it prefabricated is likely the simplest option and it will only cost you a few thousand to have it done.

That sounds expensive but you can be sure the container is insulated, reinforced, and that the doors and windows will work. On the other hand; putting in a door or window is not hugely difficult on your own if you have the correct tools and enough grit to see the job through. A grinder and a torch will make an easy job of putting in a door frame or window.

If you want a more complicated structure, then clearly having a generic door and window put in place will not serve you that well. You can pay to have it custom built, but 'custom built' is always going to cost a lot more. Custom building will often be charged per container so it may turn out that building them on-site will work out more cost effective.

Containers usually flex thanks to their fairly thin walls, so this means a normal window or door might not cut it once in place. Buying this is easy enough but you do need to be sure you are using the correct doors and windows. Ask a professional before buying to avoid disappointment.

If you are just going to cut out windows and doors, then most containers will be fine structurally. If you are going to cut out entire walls you will need to start putting in proper supports or beams to support the structure.

If you want to have more space but you are not too keen on building a very complex structure with lots of supports and structures, then you might consider having a few separate units. This will require you to wire and put piping in for each one, but this may be easier overall.

Walls and framing

If you plan to live in your shipping container, then corrugated steel walls may not be the best option for living with either practically or mentally. Putting in a wooden frame and paneling is fairly simple and allows for insulation that many people will be comfortable doing themselves.

One of the big questions will be how you choose to attach the framing to your container. Since the walls are not particularly thick you could end up with unsightly bolts all over it if you are note careful.

You have two main solutions if you are concerned about this (and if they are going to be getting serious weathering it might be more than an aesthetic issue). You will need to be sure that any external screws or bolts are treated to be weatherproof.

Firstly, you can hide them by putting an exterior onto the container or using strategically placed decorations to make sure nothing can be seen. Any roof you put in can be used to cover some of the most glaring bolts.

Secondly you can find a way of attaching the frame without using bolts through too much of the container. You could do this by gluing brackets to the ceiling and using a very strong bolt to the floor. Spray foam will often do a good job of attaching dry wall to the container. Welding might even be an option for some of the framing.

The frame can be safely attached to the floor and steel wall and then covered with a paneling of your choice including wooden planks or drywall. Be sure to put in any wiring before you start finishing off this section of your home.

Floor

The floors of shipping containers are often treated with chemicals to keep out pests and vermin and means they often need to be treated themselves. The risk is usually minor and not too significant if you are just using the container for storage or brief periods of time, however it's probably not a great idea to sleep on top of a floor that has been treated with deadly poison for too long.

Most people choose to renovate their floor by washing them down with a good cleaner and placing basic wooden subflooring on top that is treated with a resin like epoxy to keep it safe. Some more radical shipping container homes might just put down a layer of concrete.

The metal panel on the front of your container should inform you what the floor has been treated with so that you can be sure of the level of work that needs to be put into it. You'll likely need to search what the different compounds are, but this will tell you what you are dealing with.

The floor of a storage container is generally not too much different than the floor of a normal home when it comes to installing paneling or carpet. If you are unsure about the floor and want to guarantee safety, then you can remove the flooring in it and replace it with your own.

Reinforcement

Before work really starts on the container you will need to put in reinforcements on the container. If you are going for a more complex or stylish design, then an engineer will have to help you determine how strong your reinforcements need to be.

The container may be strong, but if you cut all the sides out then like any structure it will fall apart. A few steel beams should be enough to hold the house up and are relatively easy to install. Things get more complicated if you are going to have several containers together with the sides completely cut out and such a structure may require more sophisticated supports.

Many popular designs of shipping containers have them as open plan structures, but you can easily place a door between containers and just have separate rooms.

Insulating a shipping container

It might seem that an incredibly sturdy box made to protect cargo on the open seas wouldn't need much insulation, but it's actually one of the most important elements of building a container home to get right.

Shipping containers have relatively thin walls and in cold climates can become incredibly soggy with condensation: especially if they are too close to the ground. If you've ever been in a tin shack in the hot sun, you'll also know what could happen if you don't have a way of cooling a container properly in the summer.

If you are in a colder environment you will need more insulation to make heating your home easier and to prevent condensation. But even in a hot environment you will need insulation to make sure cold air stays in, and if it's really hot to make sure you can use air condition properly.

Inside insulation

If you are using a wooden stud frame in your home, then you have quite a few options to help keep things insulated between the frame and the container. Most people will recommend using spray foam for a job like this: especially if you are going to be doing it DIY.

A spray foam is very easy to apply (messy too, but not particularly dangerous like other options), and if done correctly will keep out moisture and keep a home warm or cool. Since in between the walls is where a lot of condensation will occur it is also the location where you will want the best insulation.

Foam comes in the cheaper open cell form which is good for keeping air in or out, but not great at guarding against moisture. Then there is the closed cell foam which is much better against vapor and water but comes with a higher price tag.

When looking for insulation it will usually be measured with an R-value that tells you about its thermal resistance and other fantastic properties. Generally, the higher the number the better the insulation of a product: though keep in mind that it's only for a bit of the material. If you more thoroughly insulate a home with a lower R-value material, you will overall be better insulated than if you did a less complete job with a better insulator.

It's not really possible to insulate a home too much and all you are doing by insulating is keeping the outside air away and letting you control movement of it. Theoretically you could insulate a house so much that it would be too cold even in summer, but that is very unlikely and would be easily solved.

If you don't want to use foam, then you can use insulation panels which are easy-to-install panels that fit in the wall. They are cheaper than spray foam, but they can get quite thick and the price can really add up if you're not careful (getting custom sized panels can make installation easy and very quick). These will be fine in dryer climates, but not do as well in wetter environments.

The cheaper alternative to this is blanket insulation such as fiberglass or rock wool which is easy to install but comes with its own risks and difficulties as fiberglass isn't the best material to handle. You do need to be careful with some of these materials, however, as they may encourage more condensation and corrosion.

These are the main types of insulations and the ones conventionally used in homes. Remember that money you save here might be lost in energy bills in the future. There are many other options as well including natural materials like wool and mud, and you can even opt for egg cartons.

Outside insulation

Insulating the inside walls is just one way of insulating your home. Placing materials on the exterior of your home can also create effective insulation and can even free up space for the inside by avoiding having to place in large walls.

If you want the quirky shipping container look you might want to avoid doing this, but there is always the option of painting the container (with a ceramic insulation paint) to keep out extra rain or to avoid absorbing too much heat.

For very cold climates outside insulation might not be optional and you can use some handsome wooden logs on the outside. This will make a cozy log cabin, in addition wooden paneling on the outside of the container can help with insulation.

Spray foam can be applied to the outside but it takes a lot more effort to protect it from the elements. If the foam is good quality and applied well then it should be fairly even, if not it might require paneling on top of it. It would then need to be coated with something like polyuria to help keep it protected.

Roof

A container comes with a roof and in certain environments it could theoretically be optional, but in most cases you will want one and it is crucial for proper insulation. Without a roof your home will drink in far more heat and can collect a lot of rainwater.

Many people in shipping containers opt for an earth room left on the flat on the container. This gives it similar qualities to a rooftop garden, the layer of soil acts as a good insulator, and in the summer it will absorb quite a bit of heat.

A normal shed style roof with corrugated sheet metal will work for many shipping containers, especially if there is not going to be a heavy load of wind or snow on the roof. A reflective metal roof will keep heat out and if you have a roof that is oversized and sloping you will have addition shade and can even encourage warm air to leave the container.

It is important that you do not make a roof that will absorb the heat into the container below so avoid absorbing colors and materials for the roof. A simple white roof can help a lot with keeping a building cool

Sealing gaps

If you don't buy a wind and rain proof container upfront and you do renovations that require cutting out large areas of wall you will need to make sure that any gaps or cracks that you make are then sealed back up to avoid letting out air where you don't want to.

You can opt for steel strips around the cracks or more traditional, and simpler, methods of filling in holes such as foam, caulk, or filler wool. Doing this will make sure your insulation methods are the most effective. It's also important that windows are double-glazed if you want very effective insulation.

The floor

Insulating the floor is one of the easiest ways to keep control of the air in your home. If you build a container home with a crawlspace, then you will have lots of space for extra wool or foam style insulation.

A subflooring that includes a damp-proof material and a sturdy floor covering; if you are looking to keep things warm then a good layer of carpet is always an easy solution to keeping things better insulated.

Things such as under-floor heating are good options, but keep in mind that heating a poorly insulated house is always costly and may ultimately not be enough to keep you warm (or cool).

Design and location

How you design and place your home is important for your energy and insulation needs. If you want to keep a home cool then simply placing it around trees will help to give it shade, and in addition can help stop strong winds and some snow cover.

Make sure that if you want to get a breeze in a home or to remove heat that will inevitably get in that you have windows that will accommodate this well, as well as vents or a good air conditioning unit. If you are going to build in a very hot environment be very careful about being too exposed or with not enough space inside. Things can get extremely hot if you aren't prepared.

In colder climates be aware that large windows will cause you to lose heater more quickly and you should try to opt for several smaller windows.

Laying the foundations

If you want to build a larger shipping container home, then you are most likely going to need a foundation of some type. What kind of home as well as what is available to you will tell you what kind of foundation you need. If you want something for storage or using as a simple workshop, then directly onto concrete or onto concrete piers might be perfectly adequate.

If you are planning on something more elaborate, then a more conventional foundation might be required. Building a very heavy home with lots of elaborate attachments might require more than a few concrete slabs if you want to be safe.

The first question is whether or not the ground you are working on is hard ground or soft soil. The softer the ground – the more elaborate and sturdy a foundation needs to be so that you can have it bear all the weight of the container.

Concrete slab

A slab-on-grade foundation is one of the most commonly used types of foundations. In short you dig a large hole into the ground and then fill this up with concrete. It's more complicated in practice but only slightly. In cold climates this won't work as well as the ground gets very cold in winter, but you can get around this with very good insulation and heating.

With this method you would be building on a giant hunk of concrete getting piping and wiring into the house can be more difficult and more expensive than if you had some space in between the ground and the container.

The slab-on-grade is what is known as a shallow foundation and there are many variations that use a similar concept of using a material relatively near the surface of the ground. This might be rubbles or iron piping: however, the slab-on-grade type is usually considered the most simply.

 For a shallow foundation to work for your home, you will need a somewhat stronger ground to work with: anything too weak can still sink or struggle to bear the desired load. It is possible to build this kind of foundation yourself if you have the correct experience.

Deep foundation

If you are using a weaker type of ground or you plan on building a very big structure, then you may need a deep foundation. There are many variations of these depending on the structure, but essentially you will place 'piles' (long and sturdy columns made a various materials) deep into the higher density ground below.

Above ground there will be columns that the load of the home is then placed on. The pile foundation can give a home an almost stilt look if you are trying to keep the home higher off the ground.

It's impossible to create a pile foundation on your own and they can be very expensive to build, so if you builder on harder ground you will be saving a lot of money initially. However, remember that putting utilities into a pile foundation home is cheaper and easier, and, in addition, the house will stay warmer easier in winter.

With this option you will have more space for a basement if you wish, but at such a point you might start to wonder why you are building a shipping container home.

Concrete Piers

As mentioned earlier you can simply use concrete piers for a home which will place six or so concrete slabs under the container to keep it up; with four on the corners and two in the middle. This is a simple solution for shipping container homes and will save you the most money and time.

Getting ready to put down the foundation

For any of these options you will need to have a report prepared about the ground you are building on. There will be soil maps available in most areas that you are looking at but they might not provide enough detail on their own.

If you are not really planning on putting much weight on a container, then most hard ground would be find as it is or with piers. The type of soil you have will let you know what strength concrete you need which is measured by its "C value" with a higher C value being a stronger concrete.

Concrete will need to be mixed and cured adequately and you will need to be cautious about the temperature when you lay down the concrete.

When your foundation is finished and you finally get your container delivered you will need to make sure it can be put in place with the space you have. If there is enough space, you can sometimes have a truck move the container directly onto the foundation without need of a crane.

If you are dealing with a smaller space, then a crane will need to be prepared to move the container over any housing that is nearby. At this point you will be thankful for any building insurance you have just in case things go wrong. Some trucks come with a smaller crane (known as a HIAB), but these can only move smaller units and vehicles.
If you have a full 40-foot container, then you will need a proper crane to move it across which will cost as much as $1,000 a day to rent and will most likely need an operator.

Containers can be bolted or welded to foundations to make sure they don't move. In general, thanks to their sturdy shape they are prone to staying still, but on the right supports they can be moved quite easily with a crowbar or similar.

Connecting the containers

If you're using more than one container, then when they are in place you will most likely need to connect them. If you wish you don't have to do this and you can use several separate containers but this can end up costing you more in walls and insulation (though it is more practical in many other ways.

If you are being truly DIY and you want the easiest option, then you can just bolt the containers together using metal plates. This is a good option as almost anyone can do it with a little bit of planning, but it's not elegant and it probably won't work for a more complex design.

The method used by most is to set two containers side-by-side after removing the sides. Reinforcing the sides and the roof and then welding them together. Sometimes pillars or a supporting wall may be required inside to ensure that the roof can be held up.

Having an open plan container with four or so containers will use a similar principle but may require pillars and will need very strong reinforcements. Putting containers end-to-end is simple to do in terms of holding them together but cutting the ends off is trickier than just the sides and has more of an impact on the structure of the container.

In some of the fancier shipping container designs, buildings are stacked on top of each other, or even placed at angles or crossed together. Clearly this is possible, but the containers are not well suited to being built like this and it requires lots of planning and reinforcements to be done.

In some ways having a two floor container home would be easier because you wouldn't need to cut out an entire wall so much as a smaller part in which to place some stairs.

The main issue with this is that it takes up a lot of space and might be quite dark; a ladder could be used if you were happy to use such an apparatus, but for the sake of simplicity side-by-side containers is usually best.

Stacking them up normally shouldn't create much of an issue structurally as they are built to do this and might not require much more reinforcement than usual. One thing you do need to be careful of though is that the bottom container is heavily reinforced if the sides are cut into as they will then lose a lot of their strength.

If you are interested in stacked container, then one popular design is to have them as almost separate apartments that you access with an external staircase.

The advantages of a shipping container come out best when you use them to make simple designs that don't put too much pressure on the walls and ceiling. When you start stacking and placing things in odd places with large structural changes then the home becomes more of a question of overcoming the container rather than working with it.

It might be worth considering combining a traditional style home with a shipping container if you especially want them stacked. You would need the help of an engineer, but doing so might help you have extra height without needing too many structural reinforcements.

There are many ways to cut the ways out including just using a grinder, but if you want neat walls, or to re-use the steel you are cutting off then hiring a plasma cutter might be your best option.

Once you have the containers set in place, the containers connect, and you have the windows and doors cut out, the walls reinforced, and the roof built you will be then ready to start finishing off the house at your own pace.

Wiring and plumbing

Wiring and plumbing should ideally be done before you have insulated the home and timed with the flooring so that you can run it through. It makes sense to having the wiring ready early on so you know how to place any other elements you haven't planned for.

Shipping container homes often lend themselves well to solar panel energy, but you do need to be prepared for the space that can take up and if you planned to use trees for shade you might want to reconsider if you need as much sunlight as possible. If you are not used to solar power, then you may need to prepare for times when there is not enough power.

There are not any particular issues or challenged when it comes to wiring a shipping container than compared to a regular house. You may need to work through some steel where containers are connected together, but if you plan ahead when you have the tools it should be easy to get around this.

A basic wiring job for a small home is not too difficult, but if you want a system done quickly that will be easily accessible in the future for maintenance then it might be worth seeking professional help to make it is done perfectly.

Plumbing the house in is a similar story and your main concern should be saving space as it will be at a premium in many designs. If you settle for a smaller wet room, then you can keep the space for the toilet and shower very minimal.

The most important thing will be ensuring that you are close enough to the sewers and grids that you can easily connect your home up. Getting your plumbing and wiring done correctly and early on can save you a lot of headache later when they require maintenance.

Creating a plan of action

Before you can start building a shipping container home you will need to have some more solid plans of action. This means knowing what you want, having the plans ready, and seeing if you can get the correct materials and help that you need.

The aim of this book has been to help you get started with planning your container home by giving you guidance and ideas so you know what is possible and what can realistically be done with various budgets.

To get started on your home you will need two plans. The actual plans that you will follow to have the home built in a way that will ensure it stands up and you don't forget to do something like putting a sink in. Then you will also need a plan of action that will take you through the process of getting the land, getting the help and tools you'll need, and finally building the home.

Here we will run through what that process might look like.

To begin you will need both the land and a plan. It's a bit tricky because they both inform each other. To buy the land you will need to show a plan of what you intend to develop, but to really have an idea of what to put in your plan and what the conditions of the land will be you need to have a better picture of the land.

Your best option when beginning is to do some research and create a rough plan. Go visit some shipping container homes or hotels around the country, or even around the world, and see what appeals to you and what is possible within a given space. Airbnb will give you numerous options to go and stay in one for a short break.

A 20-foot shipping container on average will have an internal area of 144 foot. You can measure that out in the space you have around you and see what would fit into it with your current furniture and life.

Once you have a handle on the real size you need to work with you can then come up with rough plans on something like Google Sketchup or use one of the sample ones later in this book (or another of your liking).

This will let you find the right land and it will just be a question of making those plans more complex and ensuring they work with the land and space you have. A realtor will be able to help you find land in the area you are looking for and should have a good idea about the zoning permission for it.

Once you've found the land and you know there is a good chance of you being allowed to build a shipping container home there, you will then need to turn to an architect or building engineer to assess the land and to help you create plans that you can take to a local council or bank to get the go-ahead with your project.

If you are building further out in the countryside and you want something that is more off-the-grid, then you may only need a quick survey to make sure the land is suitable to build a home with a simple foundation on.

Once you have the finalized plans and enough information about the land you are building on you can start looking to buy the containers. You will need to choose if you want to inspect them and how much you want to have built off-site. You can have a practically finished home placed onto your foundations and have it finished in a matter of days.

To go from container to home you will need to firstly renovate the container so that it will not get weather damage while it is being built (though you may not want to do too much, too early on as you are likely to be making adjustments). Once the foundation is in place (based on how soft the ground is) you will have the containers placed on it, bolted or welded into place, and then joined together.

At this stage you will need to reinforce the containers before cutting out walls or spaces for windows and doors. With that done you can start to focus on the floor and roof – making sure the roof will be weatherproof and the floor does not pose a threat to your health.

Depending on your insulation method you would next need to either lay down the spray insulation, or put up a stud frame and put the insulation in around it (if you are insulating mostly from the interior).

With framing, insulation, and the floor done you will most likely want to start installing the wiring and plumbing for the home in the correct locations (if you put all the water sources together you will save space). Prior to this you will need to make sure you have permission to connect to the sewers and electricity grid, and the facilities are in place to have this done.

Now you are free to either finish off paneling the interior or painting and beautifying the exterior. All external bolts or metal must be treated so they are weatherproof and will not allow in any moisture. If you are going to be putting in vents this would be a good time to do it.

With the outside done you can put in windows and doors and finish off the inside. You are then left with the task of painting, decorating, and furnishing your home.

Getting the right help

When you design a shipping container you will need to make sure that the help you get knows what they are doing and ensure they are used to dealing with modular homes, and especially if they know how to work with shipping container homes.

Having the right people on your side can save you a lot of time and energy. If you end up paying a little extra for the right expertise you may have ultimately avoided losing money in other areas. Whether that is fixing problems that were created, spending time getting several people where one might have managed, and in getting invaluable advice.

Companies exist that specialize in this kind of work and if you stick with them for the whole project they can help you with planning, insurance, management, and funding. However, they will charge you a lot for this and it's up to you to determine if that is a fair price.

You will need to make a choice over how much work you want to put into a shipping container home. There are lots of elements that a relatively handy person would be comfortable doing such as large parts of the interior, but not all of us are quite so handy with a plasma cutter or a welding torch.

If it is a small build and you are confident at working, then you may be able to get away with just getting help laying the container and having the more precise elements done for you. If you are going to require a lot more help then getting an experienced contractor to guide you through the process can save you time, and even ultimately money.

If you have everything planned out well then you can save money by having contractors do multiple jobs while they are on-site and to avoid paying them to stand around waiting for something to be delivered.

It is worth figuring out how much it would cost you to have some tasks do on-site or off-site as small welding jobs might work out cheaper off-site, even if you are charged a little more per task than hiring a welder yourself might cost.

When hiring a contractor try to make sure they have experience with shipping containers or at the very least with modular homes. If you are struggling to find one, then find shipping container builds in your area and ask who helped build them.

Taking the time to find the right contractor will help you significantly in the end. Don't always go for the cheapest contractor as that too may not be the most effective route and always work out a solid contract before going too far ahead with the work.

Example plans

Now that you have the groundwork in place to start designing and preparing to build a shipping container home, what's left is to start looking at plans. In the following section there are several container home plans for you to look at either for inspiration or to act as the basis for your own plans.

Having your own custom plans professional created is entirely feasible, but one of the real strengths of a shipping container home is that most plans will follow a fairly strict set of conventions. Since most containers are a similar size you will be working with similar materials and similar sizes.

Unless you have a very particular idea of how the building should look pre-designed plans should be more than adequate in getting the home you want. When deciding on a plan try to consider the costs they will incur before you get too trenched in to an idea.

The simpler a design is, the more likely you can have it built quickly and cheaply. For a shipping container home, a very basic design may not even require a proper plan if you are an experienced builder.

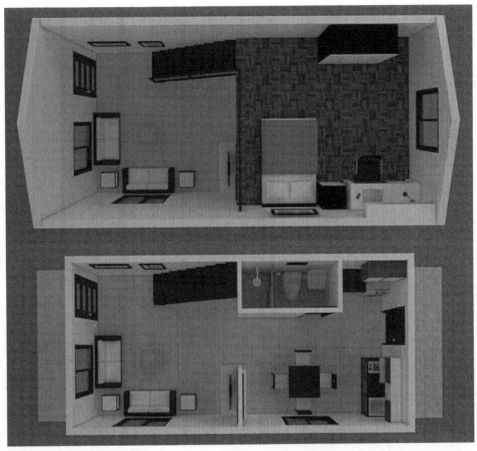

Plan A: Lofty Heights

This is a very simple plan and gives you a good idea of what you can accomplish with a smaller box-shaped home. As you can see several spaces become multiple spaces with the dining room being used for many of your general space needs.

This kind of container home would require at least two containers to have enough space, and you might consider doubling down on this design by removing the dining room and separate laundry space entirely.

A loft space for a bedroom is a very clever way of making the most out of your space, but to do this with a container home you would need to consider stacking the containers or having heightened containers with room for a loft bedroom.

There would be easy ways to make more of your space than this plan allows. A smaller loft that was accessed by a ladder over the kitchen would mean you wouldn't have to find space for a bedroom (which often has lots of unused space in conventional homes) and you won't notice it encroaching on your headspace when you are relaxing or eating in the living room.

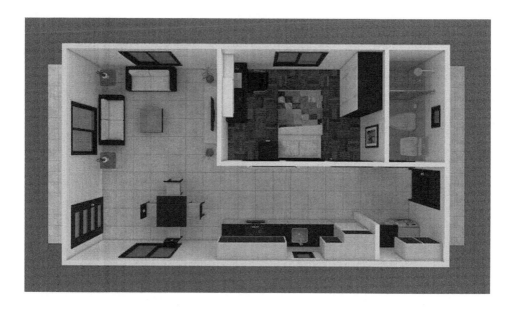

Plan B: A simple home

This is one of the simplest designs you can get for a shipping container home and contains all of your living in needs in a very functional, but still livable space.

Again there is lots of room for shaving off space here, including making the bathroom into a smaller en-suite space and forgoing a dining space altogether. It would really be a question of whether you favored space or having furniture.

It's tempting to put in space for an office and a dining room, but you can often make do with a good quality coffee table and an extended kitchen with a smaller breakfast bar.

One of the perks of this design is that it uses the original walls of the container to give the bedroom extra privacy, and in turn that will make the structure sturdier and require fewer reinforcements and supports.

The most appealing feature is arguably that getting it in place and working on the structure is one of the easiest approaches possible.

Plan C: Zig-Zag

A design like this is easy to build than it might first appear and benefits from the fact that not as many of the walls need to be cut out or removed. In fact, if you wanted to keep cutting and pulling apart you could just put a single door between the two containers.

The container would not feel as airy or light this way, but you would save some time and money (although you would need to build more ways, and put in more insulation.

This design really helps to add more space to a container home because the living room and bedroom feel further apart and are given more privacy.

Open plan is a good way of making the most of a smaller space, but it can also lead some homes into a sense they are too simple and they don't allow you to compartmentalize your life as successfully. You might also find this kind of design is easier to keep heated and you can safely cook-up a storm in the kitchen without stinking out the whole house.

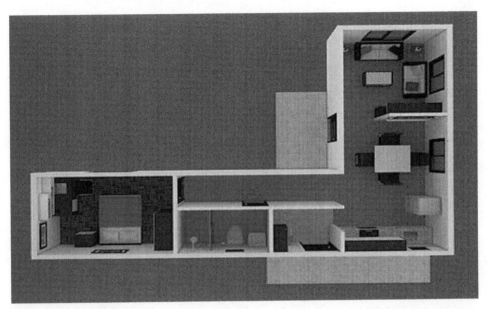

Plan D: The L- Shape

Having your shipping containers arranged in this way means you start to get the best of both worlds. You get the openness of an open plan living set-up, but you also get some more privacy and a feeling of depth in the home.

Again you can choose to keep thing more simply by just placing a door between two different containers here, or even opening them up with a transparent wall and a glass door.

One thing that makes this particular design so successful is that it allows you to interact with the outside space more by putting it right at your fingertips. You can add large windows to look outside and even put a shelter outside for a dining area that will then free up space inside. In addition, there is maximum privacy for the bedroom.

The big downside is that you don't make the most of an open plan space and you end up with narrower rooms than might otherwise have been desired.

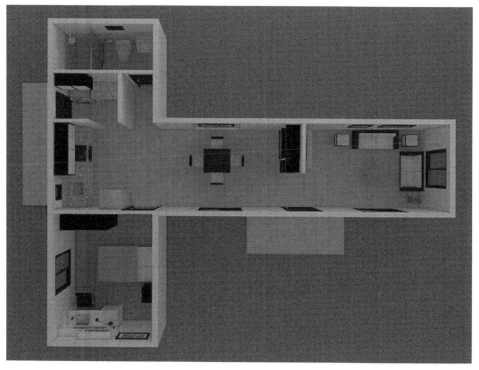

Plan E: The T-Shape

As with the last design this one makes a good compromise between space and privacy, but arguably you lose a little less space where the containers meet. This is quite an easy to design to carry out because it doesn't require huge amounts of reinforcement.

What this design does give you is a lot of outside space to turn into living space with relative ease. This can really create extra space in a small living environment and give a sense of lightness and openness. If you are not careful then shipping containers can be dark and dingy on the inside.

The main issue is that it's not the most efficient use of space and you may struggle to be given permission for a t-shaped home in a lot of locations. If you can carry out this design it can be truly stylish and use your land well.

Conclusion

With the information here you should be well on your way to planning your shipping container home and making your dream a reality. A shipping container is one of the cheapest and easiest ways to have a modern and stylish looking home without a huge price tag.

They come off the boat with the perfect shape for a modular home and you should feel free to take full advantage of that. With these unique strengths and space for customization come unique challenges. They require extra insulation, they can be dark if you don't put in enough opportunities for space, and the ways only remain strong so long as they aren't cut into.

These obstacles shouldn't be seen as too off-putting however, as any home comes with its own hardship and if you are interested in a shipping container home they will seem like minor issues once it is complete.

This is your new home and you should be proud that you have used a structure that is environmentally friendly and makes clever use of materials that might otherwise have been thrown away. The shipping container home may naturally be small in space, but it comes with more life than your typical home.

Printed in Great Britain
by Amazon